INTRODUCTION

The Captain Cook Country Tour will take you on a journey of discovery as it follows the life of Britain's most famous seaman and explorer.

It will take you through a variety of landscape: from industrial activity, through moorland and to the rocky coastline from which James Cook took his inspiration.

Much of the countryside has not changed for hundreds – or even thousands – of years. You can share the same views which Cook saw as he explored the countryside around his childhood home.

You will find his schoolroom and trace the tracks he followed on his way to his first job at Staithes.

The rugged coastline still maintains all its grandeur which impressed the young Cook, and the changing sea will excite and thrill even the most timid of those who follow this tour around Captain Cook Country.

MOORLAND SOLITUDE

COOK'S BIRTHPLACE MUSEUM

STAITHES AND BOULBY CLIFFS

THE ROUTE

The tour is a circular route of around 70 miles (113km) with roadsigns from Marton, in Middlesbrough to Whitby. You can join the tour at any point although this booklet describes the route from Marton which is the logical starting point if you follow Cook's early story from his birthplace.

The tour can be completed by car in a whole day, but to take full advantage of the Cook-related museums and attractions, the opportunities for short walks and soaking up the special atmosphere of Cook Country, you may wish to spend two or more days on your voyage of discovery. You could leave the main route at any point to enjoy the local towns, villages and countryside. Accommodation of every type and price range is available en-route.

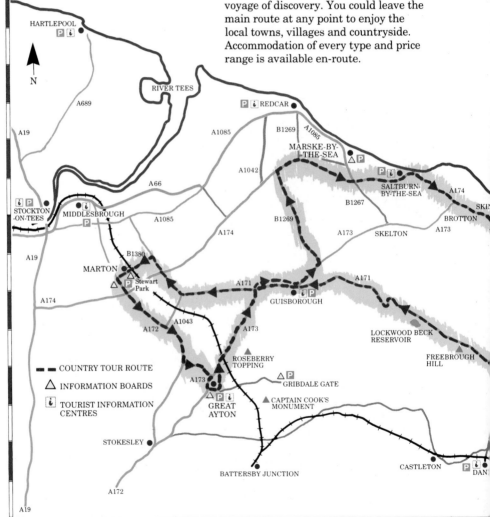

Please take care on the roads: you will share them with many other users, including cyclists, horse riders, walkers, tractors and sheep.

AN INHERITANCE FOR THE FUTURE

We hope you enjoy the tour and will help those who live and work here in protecting our heritage for future generations.

Please respect the privacy of those who live in the places you will visit. Take any litter home with you.

The tour is accessible by public transport which offers a way of enjoying the route without the problems of parking, petrol or pollution. There is also a Cook Country Walk for those who wish to discover the countryside on foot.

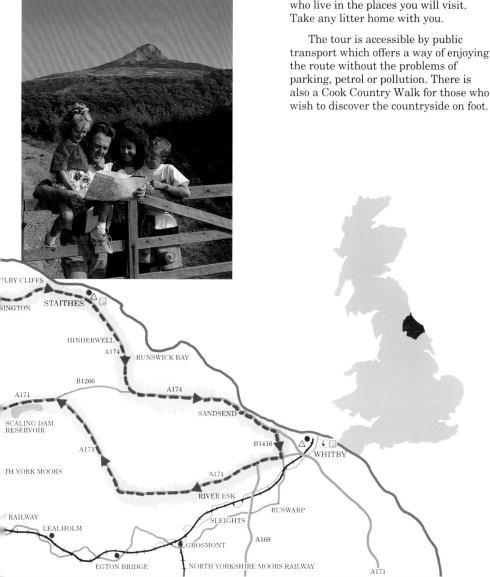

MARTON TO GREAT AYTON

1 The Cook Birthplace Museum, Marton, Middlesbrough

The tour starts at this award-winning museum where special effects tell the story of Cook, his naval career, voyages of discovery and his world-wide influence. The museum opened in 1978 and is set in the 114 acres of Stewart Park. In addition to lakes and a children's zoo, there is a large conservatory full of tropical plants many of which first became known to the western world thanks to Cook and his botanical colleagues on board the Endeavour and Resolution.

A few yards from the museum a large granite vase erected by Bolckow, the iron master in 1858 marks the site of the low, thatched cottage where Cook was born on 27th October 1728. The cottage was demolished in 1786 to make way for a mansion which was subsequently destroyed by fire.

Cook's father was a day labourer employed on local farms, a fairly insecure job which reflected the seasons and the local economy. He had come from Scotland and married Grace in the nearby village of Stainton in 1725. James, their second child, was baptised at St Cuthbert's Church, Marton on 3rd November 1728.

MARTON IN MIDDLESBROUGH TO GREAT AYTON

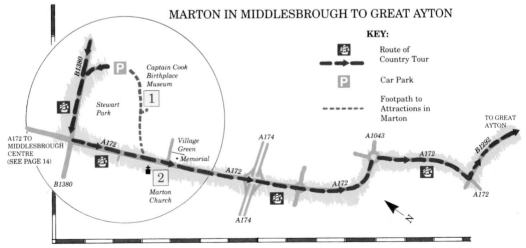

KEY:

- Route of Country Tour
- **P** Car Park
- Footpath to Attractions in Marton

ALONG THE WAY

Ormesby Hall lies just to the east of Stewart Park, a Georgian mansion erected by Dorothy Wake, daughter of an Archbishop of Canterbury, in 1740. Cook's father worked on the estate when the family lived in Ormesby. The interior decorations are particularly interesting as is the adjacent stable block. The property is owned by the National Trust.

Roseberry Topping dominates the Cleveland landscape. The natural outcrop has been eroded since Cook walked its tracks. Both quarrying and natural landslips have changed its profile, which was once suggested as the ideal place to erect a memorial to Cook.

2 Marton Church

Since the infant Cook was brought to St Cuthbert's church over 250 years ago the building has been rebuilt and restored several times to make it more relevant to the needs of the community. In 1728 the church was a plain, whitewashed building with parts of the original Norman church and additions of 1630.

Look at the register for 1728 and you see just another entry - 'James the son of James Cook day labourer baptized' - written in a simple hand which did not know how this tiny child would become a legend in his own lifetime, and a person respected the world over a couple of hundred years later.

The register is now housed in a display cabinet made in the village of

Kilburn near Thirsk by Robert Thompson's Craftsmen. Look for their trademark of the carved mouse: there are other mice on woodwork elsewhere in the church if you look carefully.

The church was restored in the 1840s at the time when Middlesbrough was just about to spread its wings. Before then, Middlesbrough was nothing more than a handful of farms and cottages on the banks of the Tees. Horizons were broad, with few hedges or trees. The land right down to the river was farmed and there were many labouring families like the Cooks.

MEMORIAL WINDOW – ST. CUTHBERT'S CHURCH

On Marton Village Green is a stone memorial from Point Hicks in Australia, the first Australian land sighted by Cook in April 1770.

As James grew up, he ran errands for the Walker family who farmed at Marton Grange. Mrs Walker taught Cook the basis of reading and writing with the aid of the family Bible.

When James was eight years old his father found a permanent post as bailiff at Aireyholme Farm, six miles away just outside the village of Great Ayton.

COOK'S BAPTISMAL RECORD

GREAT AYTON TO MARSKE

3 Great Ayton

The move to Great Ayton brought Cook to a village which boasted a school. His father's employer, Thomas Skottowe, paid for James to attend the village school where he added arithmetic to his knowledge.

GREAT AYTON TO MARSKE

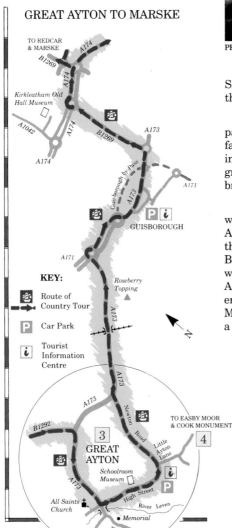

KEY:

🏛 Route of Country Tour

🅿 Car Park

ℹ Tourist Information Centre

PEACEFUL GREAT AYTON

The school is now the Captain Cook Schoolroom Museum which celebrates the life of Cook and the locality.

Elsewhere in the village is the old parish church (All Saints). The Cook family regularly attended All Saints and in the graveyard you will find the graves of Cook's mother and five of his brothers and sisters.

Although James left the village when he was 16, the family remained at Aireyholme Farm until 1755, building their own cottage of stone and brick in Bridge Street, Great Ayton. This cottage was dismantled and shipped to Australia in 1934 where it was re-erected in Fitzroy Gardens in Melbourne. The site is now marked with a granite memorial.

THE SCHOOLROOM MUSEUM

ALL SAINTS CHURCH

COOK'S FAMILY COTTAGE –
NOW IN MELBOURNE

Much of Great Ayton is now a conservation area, with the River Leven and the spacious greens enhancing the peaceful scene. In the 18th and 19th centuries all was not so tranquil with village industries as varied as tile making, brewing, tanning and weaving.

4 Easby Moor

A diversion to Gribdale and a walk to the Cook Monument on Easby Moor is well worth considering. A four mile circular walk takes in the sharp, pointed hill of Roseberry Topping which has dominated the Cleveland skyline for thousands of years. The walk also goes past Aireyholme Farm where Cook's father worked, and up to the Monument, erected in 1827.

ALONG THE WAY

Guisborough was the ancient capital of Cleveland and site of an Augustinian Priory. The Priory was founded by Robert de Brus in 1119 and is open to the public (English Heritage).

Kirkleatham has a superb group of 18th century buildings including almshouses built in 1676 and a splendid museum.

Redcar has various connections with the Cook family and amongst its many attractions is 'The Zetland', the oldest surviving lifeboat in the world, built in 1800.

MARSKE TO STAITHES

5 Marske

Cook's father left Great Ayton in his old age to live with his daughter at Redcar. He died six weeks after his son was killed in Hawaii in 1779, without ever hearing the news. He was buried on 1st April 1779 at St Germain's Church, although his grave was for many years unmarked.

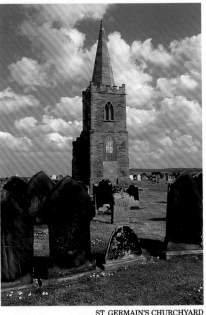

FISHING BOATS AT MARSKE

ST. GERMAIN'S CHURCHYARD

St Germain's Church was a landmark for sailors and fishermen, but the church was largely demolished in 1960, leaving the solitary tower standing guard over the grave.

6 Staithes

Old Staithes and Cowbar (on the northern bank of the beck) cling to the cliffs like limpets. But over the years storms and more steady erosion have taken their toll, washing many cottages into the sea including several which Cook would have known.

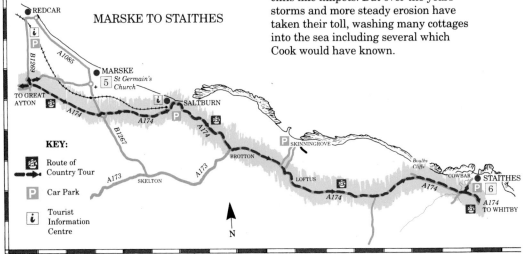

MARSKE TO STAITHES

REDCAR

B1269

A1085

MARSKE
5 St Germain's Church

TO GREAT AYTON

A174

SALTBURN

A174

B1267

A174

SKINNINGROVE

A173

SKELTON

A173

BROTTON

LOFTUS

A174

Boulby Cliffs

COWBAR

STAITHES
P 6

A174
TO WHITBY

KEY:

Route of Country Tour

P   Car Park

i   Tourist Information Centre

N

in 1746 Cook journeyed down the coast to Whitby where he was apprenticed to John and Henry Walker whose coal vessels plied up and down the east coast.

Village life at the time young James worked here is depicted in life-size street scenes of 1745 – created in the Captain Cook and Staithes Heritage Centre in the former Primitive Methodist Chapel on the High Street.

"COOK'S COTTAGE"

Cook was 16 when he came to work in William Sanderson's general store. No doubt his brief schooling in Marton and Great Ayton helped get him the position: Cook's eagerness to learn arithmetic and writing had already earned him respect amongst his elders.

Sanderson's shop played an important part in the life of the busy port. Most of the villagers worked in the fishing industry, either out in the boats or gutting and salting fish. Cook would have heard many tales of the sea and seamanship as customers came and went, or sat mending nets waiting for better weather.

The shop where Cook worked has long ago slipped into the sea although it is said that parts were salvaged and used in the building now known as Cook's Cottage.

ALONG THE WAY

Saltburn is a peaceful Victorian resort where you can still ride from the town down to the pier on the oldest remaining water balance cliff lift in Britain. Nearby at the Saltburn Smugglers you can hear stirring tales of the smugglers' coast.

Boulby Head is the highest point on England's east coast. Early Alum works of 1615 have given way to the huge mine which extracts potash from hundreds of feet below the sea bed.

Cook's interest in the sea and ships developed over the years he spent in Staithes. Some stories say that Cook abruptly left the shop after being accused of mislaying – or stealing – a shilling. What is more likely is that his employer encouraged Cook's interest in the sea and seamanship. Whatever the reasons,

SALTBURN-BY-THE-SEA

BOULBY HEAD

STAITHES TO WHITBY

7 Whitby

Make for the Cook statue on
Whitby's West
Cliff. Here you
have a
panoramic
view of all that
makes Whitby
what it is: the
ancient Abbey
and squat St
Mary's Church
face you across
the harbour;
the pantiled
roofs of
cottages rise

OVERLOOKING THE HARBOUR

from the waterside; the fish quay and
lifeboat; yet the sea dominates
everything, just as it did almost 250
years ago when Cook arrived here.

According to local tradition Cook
lived on the east side, just over the
bridge in Grape Lane. It was here that
John Walker had his house and Cook
stayed in a room on the top floor during

COOK MEMORIAL MUSEUM

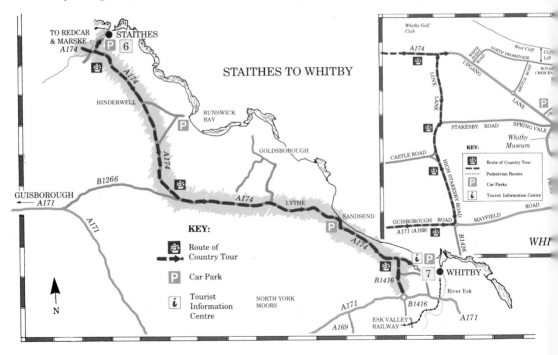

STAITHES TO WHITBY

KEY:

- Route of Country Tour
- P Car Park
- i Tourist Information Centre

KEY:
- Route of Country Tour
- Pedestrian Routes
- P Car Parks
- i Tourist Information Centre

ALONG THE WAY

Hinderwell takes its name from St Hilda's Well, a spring in the churchyard which St Hilda is said to have blessed in the 7th century. Cook probably worshipped here as William Sanderson, his employer in Staithes, was Church Warden at Hinderwell Parish Church. The church was largely rebuilt in 1773 and the tower added in 1817.

Runswick Bay is a pleasant, sheltered village at the foot of a steep bank. The picturesque jumble of cottages and gardens makes this one of many places where the click of cameras all but drowns out the cry of the seagulls.

Goldsborough is a tiny hamlet perched on top of the cliffs. It was the site of a Roman signal station, part of a sophisticated network erected to pass messages along the eastern coast.

Lythe is 500 feet above sea level and commands fine views over the sea. The church of St Oswald is still a landmark for sailors, whilst the private Mulgrave Castle lies hidden in a beautiful position in the woods. In 1775 Sir Joseph Banks, the botanist who had accompanied Cook to the Pacific, visited Mulgrave with Omai, a Tahitian who had been brought to England in almost the same way as the plant specimens and botanical drawings.

FISHING BOATS AT RUNSWICK BAY

Lythe Bank (1 in 4) leads down to Sandsend with its long stretch of sand leading all the way to Whitby.

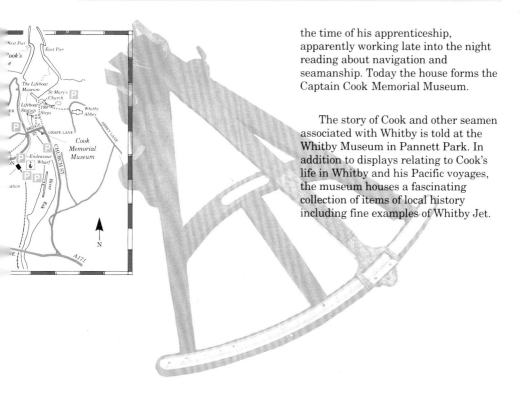

the time of his apprenticeship, apparently working late into the night reading about navigation and seamanship. Today the house forms the Captain Cook Memorial Museum.

The story of Cook and other seamen associated with Whitby is told at the Whitby Museum in Pannett Park. In addition to displays relating to Cook's life in Whitby and his Pacific voyages, the museum houses a fascinating collection of items of local history including fine examples of Whitby Jet.

When he was in port, Cook would have climbed the 199 steps on his way to worship at St Mary's Church. The climb is not any easier today, but well worth the effort. The Abbey ruins are perhaps some of the most photogenic in the country and St Mary's Church, although altered since Cook's days, is fascinating with its box pews, triple decker pulpit and galleries.

Up river was Fishburn's Shipyard, where vessels used by Cook on his famous voyages were built. They were sturdy ships which could trace their ancestry to the coal carrying ships in which Cook regularly sailed between the Tyne and London.

During Cook's early years, Britain used its wealth and naval power to win colonies. But the rivalry with France and Spain kept the Royal Navy on its toes. In Spring 1755, Cook left his ship which was anchored in the Thames and volunteered to serve on the frigate Eagle.

The following year France and Britain were at war and within the space of a few years he worked his way from able seaman to master of his own vessel. Over the next twenty years he made a name for himself as marine surveyor and navigator, laying the basis of world-wide knowledge of the Pacific Ocean from Arctic to Antarctic.

ST. MARY'S CHURCH – 199 STEPS FROM THE TOWN

WHITBY'S MAJESTIC ABBEY RUINS

His name is recorded on maps from Alaska to New Zealand, but nowhere is it spoken with such pride as in this part of north east England.

WHITBY'S COLOURFUL HARBOUR

WHITBY TO MARTON

The return to Marton is across the northern edge of the North York Moors National Park, England's largest area of heather moorland.

The road keeps to the high ground, but below lies the Esk Valley with a score of attractive villages. Roads into the valley are very steep and the best way to see all of the valley is from the Esk Valley Railway Line. At Grosmont this links with the North Yorkshire Moors Railway, an 18 mile steam-hauled line running over the moors to Pickering.

RALPH CROSS

STEAMING TO PICKERING

ALONG THE WAY

Freeborough Hill, rising to 821 feet, was said to be the burial mound of King Arthur but is a natural formation similar to Roseberry Topping.

Nature's World at the Botanic Centre at Acklam near Middlesbrough is a unique environmental centre demonstrating aspects of organic gardening, recycling and environmental awareness.

MOORLAND STANDING STONES

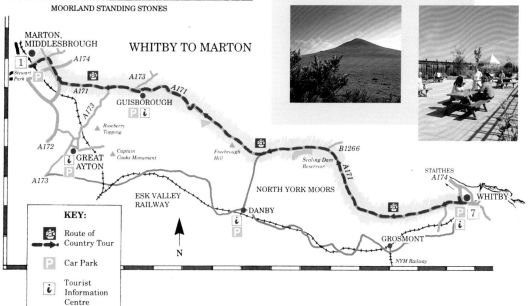

KEY:

- Route of Country Tour
- P Car Park
- ℹ Tourist Information Centre

NEXT PORT OF CALL

Middlesbrough

In Cook's day Middlesbrough was no more than a collection of farms and cottages on the south bank of the wide River Tees.

A hundred years later a group of businessmen led by Edward Pease of

THE "BOTTLE OF NOTES"

Darlington bought 500 acres of land with the intention of building a port to ship Durham coal. From this beginning one of Britain's fastest growing towns expanded through the 19th century as public buildings, houses, churches and industry developed.

TRANSPORTER BRIDGE – SPANNING THE TEES

The iron industry dominated the region until replaced by chemicals and steel, a story told at the Dorman Museum in Linthorpe Road. During the 1980s and 1990s much of the face of Middlesbrough has changed, with new public buildings and open spaces, earning it a role as a regional centre for business and shopping.

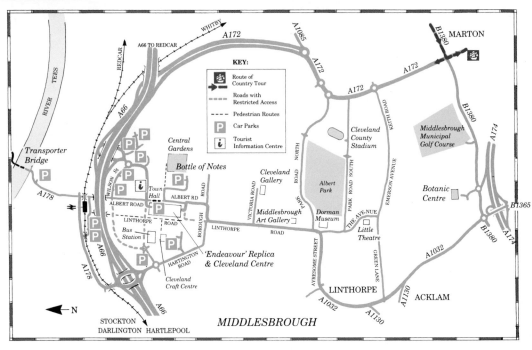

Although the tour ends back at the birthplace of Cook at Marton, there is a one fifth scale replica of the Endeavour in the Cleveland Shopping Centre, and the most recent tribute to Cook is a 32 feet (10m) high sculpture by the international artists Claes Oldenburg and Coosje van Bruggen. Created out of the script from Cook's journals and called the 'Bottle of Notes', you can find it in Central Gardens, Middlesbrough.

"ENDEAVOUR" IN THE CLEVELAND CENTRE

Hartlepool

Maritime history is recreated at Jackson Dock in Hartlepool's new marina development. Here you can see the new Historic Quay visitor attraction which relives the era of Nelson and Napoleon and includes the HMS Trincomalee, the oldest British warship afloat as well as a growing number of traditional North East sailing craft.

Stockton

A full sized replica of the Endeavour is the centrepiece of the Castlegate Quay Heritage Project on the northern bank of the River Tees.

STOCKTON'S CASTLEGATE QUAY

HARTLEPOOL'S MARINA

COOK BOYHOOD WALK

From Gribdale Gate car park, the route climbs gradually to Cook's Monument, descends Larners Hill and then follows a tarmac lane to Aireyholme Farm. From there a track passes Roseberry Topping, allowing the more ambitious walker to climb to the summit, before turning to climb the escarpment of Little Roseberry. The final section of the route follows the edge of the escarpment to return to Gribdale. Walkers arriving at Great Ayton Station may join the route at the crossroads 1/4 mile up Dikes Lane.

James Cook was born at Marton in Cleveland, went to school in Great Ayton and lived for some years at Aireyholme Farm - all within sight of Roseberry Topping.

During his early years, Cook must have spent many hours walking in this area, no doubt often climbing to the summit of Roseberry and following the escarpment to Gribdale and Easby Moor.

There have been a number of dramatic changes in the landscape since Cook's childhood. Between 1760 and the 1920s extensive mines and quarries were opened in the district for the exploitation of alum, jet, iron ore, roadstone and building stone. The waste tips, mine adits and overgrown railway routes are still to be seen. New roads and buildings have been constructed and in 1861 the present railway line was built. Cook could not, of course, have viewed the monument on Easby Moor erected in 1827, nor would he have seen the extensive coniferous forests planted since the First World War.

Farming patterns have changed over the past 200 years, as has the management of the moorland areas. The basic shape of the land, however, has changed little since Cook tramped these hills, and today we can follow his

THE CLEVELAND HILLS AT EASBY MOOR

footsteps and contemplate the scene he observed on his boyhood walk.

There are superb views of the vale of the Tees, though they are very different from those Cook enjoyed. Even 100 years after Cook played on these moors, the scene was largely pastoral. Ord's History of Cleveland (1846) describes the scene:

"The prospect from the summit combines at once the extreme of beauty and sublimity. Nature in her loveliest and most majestic attire; mountains, moors, rivers, ocean, with a vast and almost absolute infinity of intermediate scenery; towns, villages, halls, castles, steeples, towers and spires - farmhouses, cottages, and simple huts - with forests, woods, groves, corn field, pastures, hedgerows, greenlanes - these, with sounds and signs of rural life and rural enjoyment, constitute one of the noblest scenes which it is possible for the mind of man to conceive ... it may be doubted, indeed, whether any scene in Europe presents equal diversity and range of prospect."

of Louisberg and the eventual storming of Quebec and the fall of French domination in Canada.

Cook remained out in eastern Canada carying out survey work and when Captain Palliser was appointed Governor of Newfoundland, Cook got his first command as master of the Grenville - his first real survey ship.

21 Dec 1762 Cook married Elizabeth Batts at Barking Parish Church in Essex.

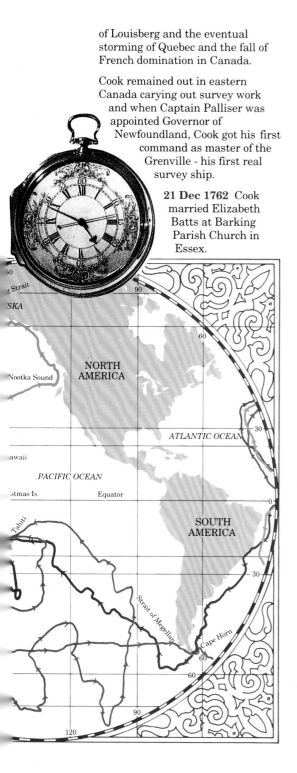

28 Aug 1768 Lieutenant James Cook RN sailed on his first voyage of discovery on board the bark Endeavour to observe the transit of Venus over the sun's disc and with secret orders which were to lead him to New Zealand.

7 Oct 1769 Cook's cabin boy - Nicholas Young - was reputed to be the first to spot New Zealand and the point was logged as Young Nick's Head. Cook started charting the coastline of the new found country and discovered it was two large islands.

A small portion of Western Australia had already been charted by Dutch voyages some 100 years before but little else was known. Leaving Australia on roughly the same latitude as the known land was plotted, Cook sailed westwards.

19 April 1770 The eastern seaboard of Australia was sighted at Point Hicks. Cook charted the coastline of Queensland and an area he first named South Wales, but later changed this to New South Wales.

28 April 1770 Cook landed in an area he originally charted as Stingray Harbour, but because of the great profusion of plants and flowers he re-named it Botany Bay.

12 July 1771 Cook returned to England in Endeavour after two years and 11 months.

——— Endeavour 1768 - 1771

——— Resolution 1772 - 1775

——— Resolution 1776 - 1780

30 Jan 1772 Now a nationally known figure, Cook returned to Whitby for a visit which was to prove his last. He also saw the family home at Great Ayton for the last time. Later in the same year, the family sold the house and today it stands in Melbourne, Australia, to where it was transhipped in 1934.

13 July 1772 The Whitby-built HMS Resolution was Cook's vessel for his second voyage of discovery on which he was accompanied by the Adventure, also Whitby-built. His task was to map out the great Southern Continent which was believed to lie around the South Pole. Cook proved it did not exist.

17 Jan 1773 Crossing the Antarctic Circle for the first time in Resolution, Cook also entered the Guiness Book of Records. Not only was he the first to cross the Antarctic Circle but he was also to become the first to circumnavigate the world in a westerly direction and the first to circumnavigate it in both directions.

21 Dec 1773 Second crossing of Antarctic Circle.

26 Jan 1774 Third crossing of Antarctic Circle which was his last and it was not crossed again for nearly half a century.

30 July 1775 Resolution returned with Cook to England and anchored at Spithead.

February 1776 Cook's memories of the 'Pembroke' crossing helped his writing of a paper on 'The Preservation of the Health of the crews of ships on Long Voyages' of which he now had great experience. For this he was elected a Fellow of the Royal Society and awarded the gold medal.

12 July 1776 The last voyage begins. Cook's third voyage of discovery was to be his last. He set sail on his promotion to Captain, with

Resolution and Discovery, the latter not joining up until 1st August. Objectives of the voyage were further exploration of the Pacific and to investigate the presence of an exit from the North West Passage.

18 Jan 1778 Cook discovered the Sandwich Islands, now the Hawaiian Islands.

7 Feb 1778 The Cook expedition crosses the Pacific eastwards to make landfall off the coast of Oregon. He turned northwards to discover Nootka Sound and British Columbia.

25 April 1778 Resolution maintains northerly heading to discover Alaska and resting for a while in what Cook charted as Anchorage Bay.

8 Aug 1778 Cook sails into the Bering Straits but needs supplies and so heads due south to Hawaii where he arrived in the November.

4 Feb 1779 Cook leaves Kealakekua Bay but forced to return because of damage to his ship.

14 Feb 1779 The party ashore was suddenly attacked by natives and Cook, along with two Royal Marines, was killed. Their remains were buried at sea on 21st February 1779.

Although world renowned as an explorer, Captain James Cook, FRS, Royal Navy, was essentially a technician and his skill as a surveyor and draughtsman were to set the seal on the quality of British prepared charts which still exists today. His work led to the formation of the Royal Navy Survey Squadrons whose charts are second to none with every ship afloat carrying its share of the Admiralty Charts.